Usborne
Little Book of
Easter Activities

Rebecca Gilpin and Fiona Watt
Recipes by Catherine Atkinson
Additional ideas by Ray Gibson

Designed and illustrated by Non Figg,
Molly Sage, Andrea Slane, Sarah Sherley-Price,
Jo Webb, Amanda Barlow, Chris Chaisty,
Michaela Kennard and Nelupa Hussain

Photographs by Howard Allman
Additional photography: Ray Moller

Contents

Pecking hens and chicks   4
Bunny wrapping paper   6
Field of rabbits   8
A chick card   10
Sheep and lambs picture   12
A chick puppet   14
Rabbit face   16
Potato-printed chicks   18
Giant spring flower prints   20
Bunny napkin rings   22
Surprise eggs   24
A bunch of daffodils   26
Easter flowerpots   28
Chicken and egg card   30
Cress egg-heads   32

Easter recipes

Chirpy chick cakes	34
Flower sweets	36
Sticky Easter cakes	38
Sunshine toast	40
Easter truffles	42
Marzipan animals and eggs	44
Easter fudge	46
Decorated eggs	48
Easter cake	50
Chocolate nests	52
Easter fruit bread	54
Spiced Easter biscuits	56
Easter daisy biscuits	58
Cheesy chicks	60
Boxes and bags	62
Easter tags	64

Pecking hens and chicks

1. Fold a paper plate in half. Open it out, then paint the back of the plate like this.

2. Fold the plate in half again. For a beak, cut a triangle from paper and glue it onto the corner.

3. Cut some triangles from brightly-coloured paper. These will be the spikes on top of the hen's head.

For a chick, instead of using a paper plate, cut around a saucer on stiff paper. Don't add the spikes to the head.

Cut feather shapes from paper and glue them on.

Tape the tail onto the
back of the plate.

4. Glue the spikes to the
back of the plate. Cut
out circles of paper and
glue them on for eyes.

5. Cut lots of thin strips of
brightly-coloured tissue
paper. Make the strips
as long as your hand.

6. Gather the strips into
a bunch and twist them
together at one end.
Tape them on for a tail.

Rock the hens and
chicks to make
them peck.

Bunny wrapping paper

Use a wax crayon.

1. Crayon lots of heads on a large piece of paper. Space them out.

2. Add two ears to each head. Draw lines inside the ears, too.

3. Use the same crayon to draw a fat body below each head.

4. Draw two feet below the bunny's body, and a wavy line for a tail.

5. Add two eyes, a nose and a curved mouth to each bunny.

6. Add whiskers. Then, colour in the bunnies with felt-tip pens.

You could try drawing a bunny like this, too.

Wrap Easter presents in your decorated paper.

6

For a gift tag, draw a bunny, then cut around it and glue it onto a piece of stiff paper. For more gift tags, see page 64.

Field of rabbits

1. Press your hand into yellow paint, then press it all over a piece of paper. Add green on top.

Paint the rabbit on top of the background.

2. When the paint is dry, dip a finger into some paint and finger paint a fat shape.

3. For a head, dip your fingertip in the paint and rub it around and around in a circle.

4. Dip a finger into the paint again and add ears. Add four legs on the rabbit's body.

5. Dip a fingertip into white paint and add a tail. Add tiny dots for eyes, too.

6. When the paint is dry, use a felt-tip pen to add a nose, whiskers and a dot in each eye.

You could use your fingertips to print flowers around the rabbits.

A chick card

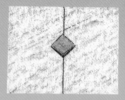

1. Cut the corner off an old envelope. Crayon all over one side of it, and inside, too.

2. Fold a piece of stiff paper in half. Crease the fold well, then open it out again.

3. Glue the corner of the envelope in the middle of the card. This makes the beak.

You could cut out half an egg shape and glue it on below your chick.

Paint streaks across some paper with a big brush. Glue on a beak when the paint is dry.

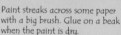

4. Lift the top of the beak. Close the card and rub across it to flatten the beak.

5. Open the card. Draw a chick around the beak. Add some eyes, legs and feet.

6. Draw flowers around the chick, or cut them out from bright paper and glue them on.

For a long card, glue body shapes over the fold, then add the beaks.

Try gluing on little pieces of tissue paper for a body.

11

Sheep and lambs picture

You don't need to wind it neatly

1. For the bodies, draw big and little wavy shapes, like these, on pieces of thin paper. Then, cut them out.

2. Dip the shapes into water. Shake off the drops, then arrange them on a large piece of paper.

3. Tape the end of some wool or yarn onto an old birthday card or postcard. Wind the yarn around and around.

Make sure both pieces of tape are on the same side.

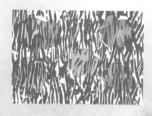

4. When the card is covered, cut off any leftover yarn. Secure the end of the yarn with a piece of tape.

5. Paint the yarn green on the side without the tape. Press it all over the paper. Add more paint as you go.

6. Gently peel off the paper bodies. When the paint is dry, add faces and legs with paint or a thick felt-tip pen.

Use a fingertip to print flowers in the grass.

A chick puppet

1. Fold three paper plates in half. Then, fold each one back the other way, along each fold.

You don't need these pieces.

2. Cut one of the plates in half along its fold. Cut a strip from the edge of one half.

Try rolling two different shades of crêpe paper together, then cut the slits (see step 7).

aint the
lates like this.

3. Mix some household
(PVA) glue with yellow,
red and orange paints.
Paint the plates.

4. When the paint is
dry, fold the two whole
plates and put them
together, like this.

5. Carefully join the
orange and red parts
together with lots of
small pieces of tape.

6. Turn the plates over
and tape the smaller
orange piece of plate
onto the red half.

7. Cut a strip of crêpe
paper as long as your
hand. Roll it tightly,
then cut lots of slits.

8. Tape the crêpe
paper roll to the back
of the yellow part. Tape
it on near the top.

9. Cut eyes from paper
and glue them on. Cut
middles for the eyes
and glue them on, too.

10. Cut a hole in a sock.
Put your hand into the
sock and push your
thumb through the hole.

11. Put your hand into
the bird, like this. Open
and close your hand to
make the bird talk.

Rabbit face

To make rabbit "ears", tie
your hair in bunches and
use hair gel to make
them stand up.

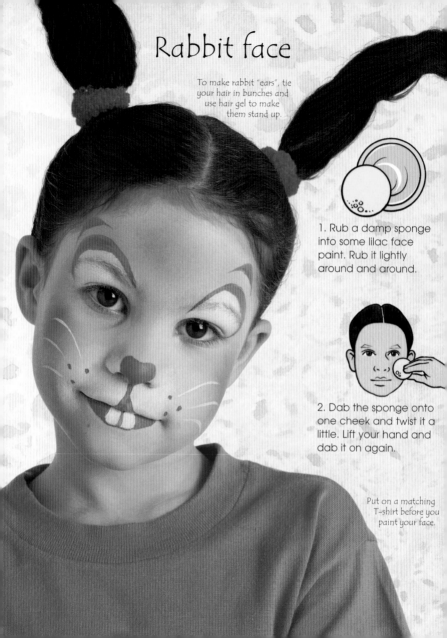

1. Rub a damp sponge
into some lilac face
paint. Rub it lightly
around and around.

2. Dab the sponge onto
one cheek and twist it a
little. Lift your hand and
dab it on again.

Put on a matching
T-shirt before you
paint your face.

If you don't have lilac face paint, you can mix other paints to make it (see below).

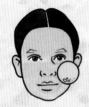

Dab the face paint over the cheeks, nose and chin. Leave a bare patch around the mouth.

4. Continue dabbing paint onto the forehead, leaving bare patches around the eyes.

5. With closed eyes and mouth, dab white face paint onto the bare patches.

. Sponge darker lilac n the cheeks and orehead. Brush on pink eyebrows.

7. Dip the brush in the pink face paint again and paint the tip of the nose, like this.

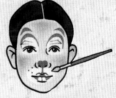

8. Paint a line from the nose to the top lip. Fill in the bottom lip. Add dots, whiskers and teeth.

Mixing paints

you don't have lilac ace paint, you can nake it by mixing ogether red, white nd blue paints.

Mix them to make purple.

1. Dab red face paint on the back of your hand. Add some blue.

2. Clean your sponge then dab on a little white to make lilac.

Potato-printed chicks

1. Lay several kitchen paper towels onto a thick pile of old newspapers.

2. Pour some bright yellow paint on top. Spread the paint with the back of a spoon.

3. Cut a potato in half. Then, cut away the two sides, like this, to make a handle.

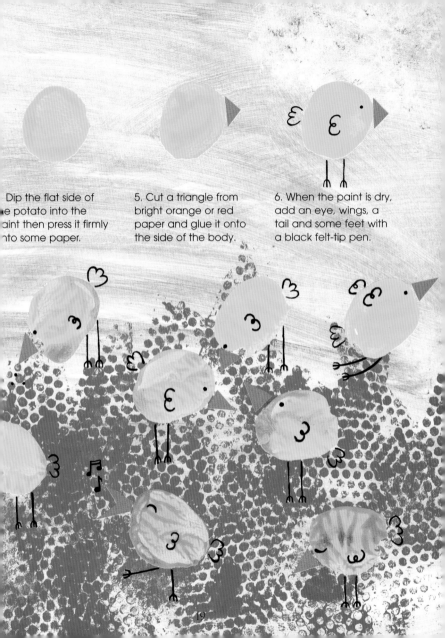

Dip the flat side of the potato into the paint then press it firmly onto some paper.

5. Cut a triangle from bright orange or red paper and glue it onto the side of the body.

6. When the paint is dry, add an eye, wings, a tail and some feet with a black felt-tip pen.

19

Giant spring flower prints

Primroses

1. Spread yellow paint onto a newspaper. Cut a small, hard pear in half and press it into the paint.

2. Press the pear onto some paper, then lift it off. Put a bottle top at the pointed end of the shape you have printed.

3. Print more pear shapes around the bottle top. Dip the pear in the paint each time you do a print.

4. Lift off the bottle top. Then, dip a fingertip into green paint. Print dots in the middle of the pear prints.

5. For big leaves, cut a large potato in half. Dip it in green paint and press it onto the paper, around the flower.

The prints on these pages are much smaller than the ones you will do.

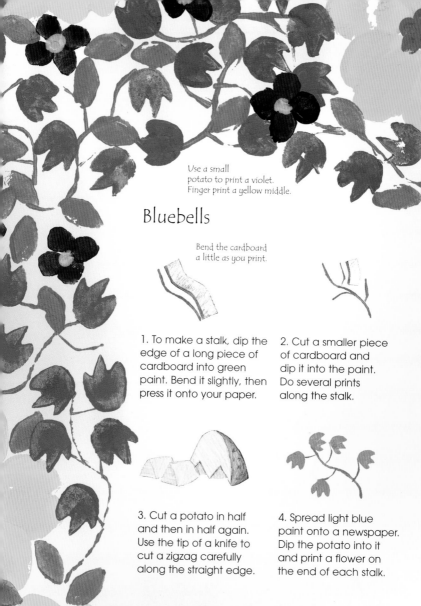

Use a small
potato to print a violet.
Finger print a yellow middle.

Bluebells

Bend the cardboard
a little as you print.

1. To make a stalk, dip the edge of a long piece of cardboard into green paint. Bend it slightly, then press it onto your paper.

2. Cut a smaller piece of cardboard and dip it into the paint. Do several prints along the stalk.

3. Cut a potato in half and then in half again. Use the tip of a knife to cut a zigzag carefully along the straight edge.

4. Spread light blue paint onto a newspaper. Dip the potato into it and print a flower on the end of each stalk.

21

Bunny napkin rings

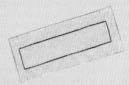

1. Take a piece of stiff paper the length of your hand and fold it in half. Draw half the shape of a bunny's head, like this.

2. Carefully cut around the shape of the head. Then, open out the paper and use felt-tip pens to draw a face.

3. For the bunny's body, draw a rectangle on a piece of stiff paper twice the length of your hand.

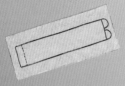

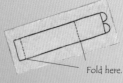

Fold here.

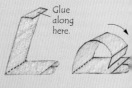

Glue along here.

4. Add two bumps on one end for the feet, like this. Draw a dotted line a little way in from the other end.

5. Draw another line a hand's length along, like this. Cut out the shape and fold it along the dotted lines.

6. Put some glue along the short edge, then curve the paper over. Stick the edge just behind the feet.

You could make these napkin rings for a special Easter meal.

Turn the head over nd put two blobs of ue below the ears. arefully, press the ead onto the body.

8. To make a tail, pull a little piece off a cotton ball. Roll it into a ball, then glue it on the back of the body.

Roll up a napkin and push it through the bunny.

To bend a bunny's ear, roll it around a pencil.

Surprise eggs

1. Trim any rough edges from around a cardboard egg carton. Paint the inside with a bright paint.

2. Turn the carton upside-down and paint the outside with the same paint. Leave the box to dry.

3. Tap the pointed end of an egg with a spoon, to crack the shell. Pull off the pieces of broken shell and tip out the inside.

4. Wash the empty shell under cold water, then leave it upside-down to dry. Crack and clean five more eggs.

5. Use crayons and food dye to decorate the eggshells. (The steps on page 48 show you how to do this.)

6. Put a tiny Easter gift, such as a small Easter egg or a toy, inside each eggshell. Put the eggs into the carton.

7. To decorate the box, fold pieces of bright cardboard. Draw half a butterfly on each piece and cut them out.

8. Close the egg box and tie a ribbon around it. Open out the butterflies and glue them onto the box.

You could hide small chocolate Easter eggs inside the eggs.

Cut flowers from wrapping paper and glue them on.

Use a felt-tip pen to add antennae to the butterflies.

Glue sequins onto the carton if you like.

You could finger print flowers all over the carton.

A bunch of daffodils

1. Draw a 12x12cm (5x5in.) square of bright yellow crêpe paper. Cut it out, then cut the square in half.

Tie a ribbon around the straws.

2. Make a frill all along one edge by stretching the crêpe paper gently between your fingers and thumbs.

3. Wrap the paper around the end of a wooden spoon. Slide it off a little and twist it into a point.

Snip each petal here.

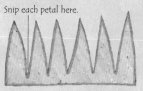

4. Fold the other piece of paper in half, short sides together. Fold it in half, then in half again. Cut it into a petal shape.

5. Open out the petals, then snip off two of the petals. Snip between each petal to separate them a little more.

6. Wrap the petals around the paper on the spoon. Wet your thumb and finger and twist the end into a point, again.

Snip here.

Cut out leaves from green paper.

7. Cut a piece off a straw, half-way down the short end. Snip the end to make two slits, like this.

8. Pull the paper off the spoon and dip the twisted end into glue. Push it into the straw and leave it to dry.

Use white crêpe paper to make narcissi. Draw along the frilled edge with an orange felt-tip pen.

9. Gently pull down each petal. Pull them a little so that they fan out evenly around the middle piece.

For a bouquet, wrap the ends of the straws in some tissue paper.

Easter flowerpots

Add mo[re]
strips if
there is
room.

1. Cut two strips of masking tape and press them on either side of a terracotta pot.

2. Cut two more strips and press them onto the pot. Press the ends inside the pot, like this.

3. Cut more strips of masking tape and press them in between the other strips.

Scrunch up the paper towel.

You can wash the paint off the eraser, later.

4. Put a little acrylic paint onto a saucer. Dip a paper towel into it and dab it between the strips.

5. Fill in between all the strips of tape. Let the paint dry, then peel off the tape.

6. Put a different paint onto the saucer, then dip an eraser on the end of a pencil into it.

Cut out flowers from wrapping paper and glue them on.

28

an Easter present,
could plant some
ng flowers in your pot.

Press the eraser
to the pot to
ake the petals of
flower, like this.

Wash the eraser,
en dip it into a
fferent shade. Add a
iddle to each flower.

29

Chicken and egg card

1. Cut a piece of stiff paper to the length of two postcards.

2. Fold the paper in half, short sides together. Open it out.

3. Fold the short sides in, so that they meet at the middle fold.

Make the egg slightly smaller than the card.

4. Draw an egg on the back of some wrapping paper, then cut it out.

Glue the egg across the middle of the card.

5. Glue the egg on the card. Draw a zigzag from top to bottom.

Don't cut the back of the card.

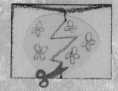

6. Pull the front and back apart and cut along the zigzag.

Decorate the inside of the card with flowers.

Draw a chick on
yellow paper. Cut it out.
Add eyes and a beak.

8. Glue the chick over
the fold in the middle
of the card.

Draw legs with a
felt-tip pen. Decorate
the inside of the card.

Use bright
wrapping
paper with
a small
pattern.

Cress egg-heads

1. Follow steps 3 and 4 on page 24 to crack the top off an egg. Fill it with cotton balls.

2. Use a spoon to pour in water. Tip the egg so that any excess water drains out.

3. Put the egg into an egg carton. Sprinkle it with half a teaspoon of cress or mustard seeds.

4. Put the egg in a light place. Add a little water every day. The cress will grow in 7-8 days.

Overlap the ends.

5. Cut a narrow strip from the short side of a postcard. Bend it around and tape it.

6. Stand the egg on top of the cardboard. Add a face with felt-tip pens and paper.

Cut out ears and glue them on for an Easter bunny.

Add a beak and wings for a chick.

Easter recipes

Chirpy chick cakes

To make 8 cakes, you will need:

50g (2oz) self-raising flour
1 medium egg
50g (2oz) caster sugar
50g (2oz) soft margarine
paper cake cases
a baking tray with shallow pans
small round sweets and jelly
diamonds or slices

For the lemon butter icing:
40g (1½ oz) butter, softened
75g (3oz) icing sugar, sifted
1 teaspoon of lemon juice (from a
bottle or squeezed from a lemon)
1 drop of yellow food colouring

Heat your oven to 190°C, 375°F, gas mark 5,
before you start.

The cakes need to be stored in an airtight
container and eaten within three days.

Decorate the chicks
with different
coloured sweets.

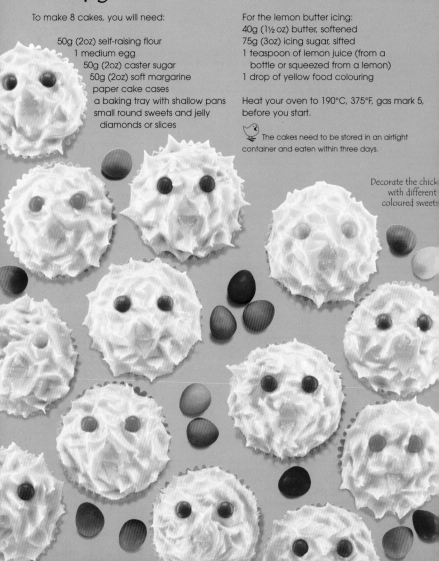

Sift the flour through sieve into a bowl. Break e egg into a cup, then dd it to the flour. Add e sugar and margarine.

2. Beat the mixture firmly with a wooden spoon, until it is light and fluffy. Put eight paper cases into pans in the baking tray.

3. Using a teaspoon, half fill each paper case with the mixture. Then, bake the cakes in the oven for 18-20 minutes.

ke the cakes until ey are golden own.

Take the cakes out f the oven. After a few ninutes, lift them out of e baking tray and put em on a rack to cool.

5. For the icing, put the butter into a bowl. Beat it with a wooden spoon until it is creamy. Then, stir in half of the icing sugar.

6. Add the lemon juice, yellow food colouring and the rest of the icing sugar. Mix everything together well.

Using a blunt knife, over the top of each ake with butter icing. hen, use a fork to make e icing look feathery.

8. Press two small round sweets onto each cake for the eyes. Then, cut eight jelly diamonds or slices in half for the beaks.

9. Press two halves into the icing on each cake, to make a beak. Make the pointed ends of the halves stick up a little.

Flower sweets

To make about 40 flowers,
you will need:

225g (8oz) icing sugar
1 tablespoon of lemon juice
   (from a bottle or squeezed
   from a lemon)
2 teaspoons egg white, mixed
   from dried egg white (mix as
   directed on the packet)
2-3 drops of lemon essence
small jelly sweets
a small flower-shaped cutter
a baking sheet

The flower sweets need to
be stored in an airtight container,
on layers of greaseproof paper.
Eat them within a week.

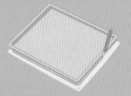

1. Put the baking sheet on
a piece of greaseproof
paper. Draw around the
tin and cut out the shape.
Put the shape in the tin.

2. Sift the icing sugar
through a sieve into a
large bowl. Make a hole
in the middle of the icing
sugar with a spoon.

*If the mixture is a little
dry, add a drop of water.*

3. Mix the lemon juice, egg
white and lemon essence
in a small bowl. Pour them
into the hole in the sugar.
Stir them with a blunt knife.

4. Keep stirring everything
together until the mixture
starts to make a ball. Then
squeeze it between your
fingers until it is smooth.

5. Sprinkle a little icing
sugar onto a clean work
surface. Sprinkle some
onto a rolling pin too, to
stop the mixture sticking.

Roll out the mixture on he work surface until it is bout 5mm (¼in) thick. hen, use the cutter to ut out a flower shape.

Put a sweet onto the iddle of the flower, and ress it down. Then, lift the ower onto the baking heet with a blunt knife.

Cut the shapes close together.

8. Cut out more flowers, one at a time, and press sweets on them. If a sweet won't stick, dab water on the flower, then press it on.

9. Press the scraps into a ball, roll it out again and make more flowers. Leave them on the baking sheet for two hours, to harden.

Sticky Easter cakes

This recipe is based on cakes that are traditionally eaten in Greece at Easter.

To make eight cakes, you will need:

100g (4oz) soft, light brown sugar
100g (4oz) butter, softened
2 medium eggs
2 teaspoons baking powder
100g (4oz) semolina
½ teaspoon of ground cinnamon
100g (4oz) ground almonds*
4 tablespoons lemon juice (from a bottle or squeezed from a lemon)
a 12-hole muffin tin

For the orange and lemon syrup:
1 small orange
1 tablespoon of lemon juice (from a bottle or squeezed from a lemon)
4 tablespoons golden syrup

Heat your oven to 200°C, 400°F, gas mark 6, before you start.

The cakes need to be stored in an airtight container and eaten within three days. Don't pour the syrup over them more than two hours before serving.

You could serve the cakes with Greek yoghurt and fresh orange segments.

Use a pastry brush.

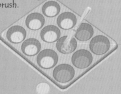

1. Brush some oil inside eight of the muffin holes. Cut a small circle of baking parchment to put in the bottom of each.

2. Put the sugar and the butter into a large bowl. Beat them together until they are mixed well and look creamy.

* Don't give these to anyone who is allergic to nuts.

Break the eggs into small bowl and beat em. Stir in the beaten gs, a little at a time, the creamy mixture.

4. Mix the baking powder, semolina, cinnamon and almonds in a large bowl. Add them, and the lemon juice, to the mixture.

5. Mix everything well, then spoon the mixture into the holes in the tin. Bake the cakes in the oven for about 15 minutes.

will be hot.

Carefully lift the cakes t of the oven. Leave em in the tin for a nute, then loosen their les with a blunt knife.

7. Turn the cakes onto a large plate to cool. Then, carefully peel the baking parchment circles off each one.

8. For the syrup, grate some rind from about half of the orange on the fine holes on a grater. Put the rind into a small pan.

Cut the orange in half. queeze out the juice, ing a lemon squeezer, nd add 2 tablespoons juice to the pan.

10. Add the lemon juice and golden syrup. Over a very low heat, gently warm the mixture, stirring it all the time.

11. When the mixture is runny, use a teaspoon to trickle it over the cakes. Let the mixture cool a little before serving.

Sunshine toast

You will need:

margarine
1 slice of bread
1 small or medium egg
a large cookie cutter
a baking sheet

Heat your oven to
200°C, 400°F, gas mark 6,
before you start.

The toast needs
to be eaten as soon as
it's cooked.

1. Dip a paper towel into some margarine. Then, rub margarine all over the baking sheet, to grease it.

2. Using a knife, spread margarine on one side of the slice of bread. Then, press the cutter into the middle of the bread.

3. Lift out the shape you have cut out. Put both pieces of bread onto the baking sheet, with their margarine sides upwards.

You can use any cutter that makes a hole that is big enough to put an egg in.

4. Break the egg onto a saucer. Then, carefully slide the egg into the hole in the bread. Put the baking sheet in the oven.

5. Bake the bread and egg in the oven for seven minutes, or for a little longer if you don't like a runny egg yolk.

Use a fish slice.

6. Wearing oven gloves, carefully lift the baking sheet out of the oven. Then, lift the pieces of toast onto a plate.

41

Easter truffles

To make 12 truffles, you will need:

225g (8oz) white, milk or plain
  chocolate drops
4 tablespoons double cream
1 teaspoon of vanilla essence
about 4 tablespoons sugar
  strands
small paper cases

The truffles need to be stored
in an airtight container in a fridge.
Eat them within five days.

1. Pour about 3cm (1in)
of water into a pan. Heat
the pan until the water
bubbles, then remove the
pan from the heat.

Wear
oven
gloves.

2. Put the chocolate
drops and cream into
a heatproof bowl. Using
oven gloves, carefully put
the bowl into the pan.

3. Stir the chocolate and
cream with a wooden
spoon until the chocolate
has melted. Carefully lift
the bowl out of the water.

. Leave the bowl to cool
or 20 minutes, then stir in
he vanilla. Put the mixture
a fridge for 1½ hours,
ntil it is very firm.

5. Put the sugar strands
onto a plate. Scoop up
some chocolate mixture
with a teaspoon and put
it into the sugar strands.

Using your fingers, roll
e spoonful in the strands
make a ball. When it is
overed, put it in a paper
ase. Make more truffles.

7. Put the truffles onto a
plate, then put them in the
fridge for 30 minutes, until
they are completely hard.
Keep them in the fridge.

To make truffle eggs,
squash the spoonful
of mixture slightly
when you roll it in
the sugar strands.

Marzipan animals and eggs

To make 4 chicks, 3 rabbits and lots of eggs and carrots, you will need:

250g (9oz) pack of marzipan*
yellow and red food colouring
toothpicks

 The animals and eggs need to be stored in an airtight container and eaten within three weeks.

Chicks

Wrap one half in plastic foodwrap.

1. Unwrap the marzipan and cut it in half. Put one half in a small bowl and add 12 drops of yellow food colouring.

2. Mix the colouring in with your fingers until the marzipan is completely yellow. Then, cut the piece of marzipan in half.

3. Put one half in a bowl and mix in a drop of red colouring. If the marzipan isn't bright orange, add another drop of red.

Keep this— piece for the wings.

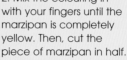

Press in two eyes with a toothpick.

4. Cut the yellow marzipan into five pieces. Make four of them into balls. Then, squeeze them at one end to make tear shapes.

5. Make eight small yellow wings and press two onto each body. Then, roll a beak from the orange marzipan and press it on.

6. For the feet, make a th orange ball and flatten i Cut the shape halfway across and open it out. Press a chick on top.

* Marzipan contains ground nuts, so don't give these to anyone who is allergic to nuts.

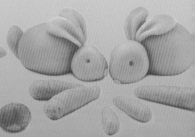

Rabbits

Use plastic foodwrap.

1. Unwrap the plain marzipan. Mix one drop of red colouring into it to make pink. Cut it in half and wrap one half.

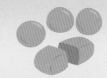

2. Cut the unwrapped piece in half. With one half, make three balls for the bodies. Then, cut the other piece in half.

3. From one half, roll three smaller balls, for the heads. Then, make six ears, three tails and three noses from the other half.

If the ears won't stick, dip the ends in water.

Pinch each ear to make a fold. Press ears, a head, a nose and tail onto each body. Then, press in eyes with a toothpick.

Marbled eggs

1. Unwrap the second piece of pink marzipan. Add a drop of red colouring, and start to mix it in with your hands.

2. Stop mixing in the colouring when the marzipan looks marbled. Roll the marzipan into lots of little egg shapes.

Use orange marzipan to make carrots. Make marks on them with a blunt knife.

Press a rabbit's head on the front of its body, to make it look as if it is lying down.

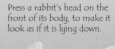

Easter fudge

To make 36 pieces of fudge, you will need:

450g (1lb) icing sugar, preferably unrefined
100g (4oz) white marshmallows
2 tablespoons milk
100g (4oz) unsalted butter
1/2 teaspoon of vanilla essence
2 drops of yellow food colouring
a shallow, 18cm (7in) square cake tin

The fudge needs to be stored in an airtight container in a fridge and eaten within a week.

Find out how to wrap your fudge like this on page 62.

1. Put the tin onto a piece of greaseproof paper. Using a pencil, draw around the tin and cut out the square.

2. Using a paper towel, wipe some oil onto the sides and bottom of the tin. Press in the paper square and wipe it too.

3. Sift the icing sugar through a sieve into a large bowl. Make a small hollow in the middle of the sugar with a spoon.

Use a spoon.

4. Using clean scissors, cut the marshmallows in half and put them in a small pan. Add the milk, butter and vanilla essence.

5. Gently heat the pan. Stir the mixture every now and then with a wooden spoon until everything has melted.

6. Pour the mixture into the hollow in the sugar. Beat everything together until it is smooth, then mix in the food colouring.

ooth the top with
back of
poon.

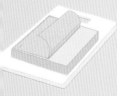

Put the fudge into the
n and push it into the
orners. When it is cool,
ut it in a fridge for three
ours to go firm.

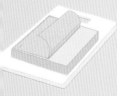

Loosen the edges of
e fudge with a blunt
nife, then turn it out
nto a chopping board.
emove the paper.

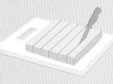

Cut the fudge into
5 pieces. Then, put
e pieces in an airtight
ontainer in the fridge
or an hour to harden.

To make
pink fudge,
use pink
marshmallows
and add a
drop of red
or pink food
colouring.

Decorated eggs

To make six coloured eggs, you will need:

6 eggs, at room temperature
food colouring
wax crayons
tiny star-shaped stickers
rubber bands

The eggs need to be stored in a fridge and eaten within three days. They can be eaten with a fresh mixed salad or on their own.

Cooking the eggs

Use a slotted spoon.

1. Put the eggs into a pan of cold water. Heat the pan until the water is gently boiling, then reduce the heat a little.

2. Cook the eggs for eight to nine minutes. Lift out one egg at a time. Cool them in a bowl of cold water for ten minutes.

Wax patterns

The wax resists the food colouring.

Leave the egg for about ten minutes.

1. Using a wax crayon, draw patterns on a dry egg. Then, put three to four teaspoons of food colouring into a glass.

2. Half fill the glass with water, then put the egg into the glass. Using a spoon, turn the egg to colour it all over.

3. When the egg is brightly coloured, lift it out of the glass with a spoon. Put the egg on a paper towel to dry.

Stickers

Make sure the egg is dry.

1. Press tiny stickers onto an egg. Use shiny ones if you can, because they don't soak up so much food colouring.

2. Colour the egg in a glass, as you did before. Then, lift the egg out with a spoon and put it on a paper towel to dry.

3. When the colouring is dry, peel off the stickers. You'll see the colour of the eggshell where the stickers were.

These rabbits and chicks were painted straight onto the eggs with food colouring.

tripes

1. Stretch a short, thick rubber band around a ry egg. Then, stretch one round the egg from the op to the bottom.

2. Add lots more rubber bands, then colour the egg and let it dry. Then, remove the rubber bands to see stripes of eggshell.

Easter cake

You will need:

225g (8oz) self-raising flour
1 teaspoon of baking powder
4 medium eggs
225g (8oz) caster sugar
225g (8oz) soft margarine
two round 20cm (8in) cake tins

For the butter icing:
225g (8oz) icing sugar
100g (4oz) unsalted butter,
  softened
1 tablespoon of milk
1 teaspoon of vanilla essence

Heat your oven to 180°C, 350
gas mark 4, before you start.

The cake needs to be stored i
an airtight container in a cool place
and eaten within three days.

To make the icing yellow,
add a teaspoon of
yellow food
colouring at
step 8.

Decorate the cake wit
flower sweets (pages 36
37) and marzipan chick
(pages 44-45

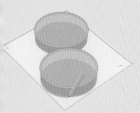

1. Put the cake tins onto a piece of greaseproof paper and draw around them. Cut out the circles, just inside the line.

Use a paper towel.

2. Wipe the sides and bottoms of the tins with a little oil. Put the paper circles inside and wipe them with a little oil too.

3. Using a sieve, sift the flour and baking powder into a large bowl. Then, carefully break the eggs into a cup.

4. Add the eggs, sugar and margarine to the bowl. Beat everything with a wooden spoon until they are mixed well.

5. Put half of the mixture into each tin. Smooth the tops with the back of a spoon. Then, bake the cakes for 25 minutes.

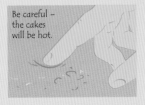

Be careful – the cakes will be hot.

6. Press the cakes with a finger. If they are cooked, they will spring back. Let them cool a little, then put them on a wire rack.

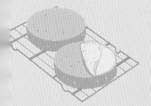

7. Peel the paper off the cakes and leave them to cool. When the cakes are cold, sift the icing sugar into a bowl.

8. Add the butter, milk and vanilla. Stir the ingredients together, then beat them until the mixture is fluffy. Put one cake on a plate.

9. Spread the cake with half of the icing. Then, put the other cake on top and spread it with the rest of the icing.

Chocolate nests

To make 10 nests, you will need:

225g (8oz) plain chocolate
50g (2oz) butter
2 tablespoons golden syrup
100g (4oz) corn flakes
30 chocolate mini eggs
paper cake cases
a baking tray with shallow pans

The nests need to be stored in an airtight container in a fridge. Eat them within three days.

1. Put ten paper cases into pans in the baking tray. Break the chocolate into squares and put them in a large pan.

The syrup slides off the hot spoon.

Try not to crush the flakes.

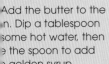

Add the butter to the [pa]n. Dip a tablespoon [in] some hot water, then [us]e the spoon to add [th]e golden syrup.

3. Heat the pan gently, stirring the ingredients all the time, until the butter and chocolate have completely melted.

4. Turn off the heat, then add the corn flakes to the pan. Gently stir them into the chocolate, until they are coated all over.

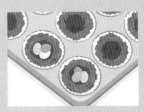

Push the flakes up the sides.

5. Fill the paper cases with the mixture. Using the back of a teaspoon, make a hollow in the middle of each nest.

6. Arrange three mini eggs in each nest. Then, put the tray in the fridge and leave it for about an hour to set.

7. Take the nests out of the paper cases and put them on a plate. Keep them in the fridge until you want to eat them.

Easter fruit bread

To make a loaf with about 12 slices, you will need:

225g (8oz) strong plain flour
1/2 teaspoon of ground mixed spice
1/2 teaspoon of salt
25g (1oz) butter
1 tablespoon of caster sugar
2 teaspoons easy-blend dried yeast
1 medium egg and 5 tablespoons milk, beaten together
100g (4oz) luxury dried mixed fruit
a little milk for brushing
a 20.5 x 12.5 x 8cm (8 x 5 x 3½in) loaf tin

For the icing:
50g (2oz) icing sugar
1 tablespoon of lemon juice (from a bottle or squeezed from a lemon)
50g (2oz) chopped glacé cherries

Heat your oven to 200°C, 400°F, gas mark 6.

Easter fruit bread needs to be stored in an airtight container and eaten within three days.

Draw around the bottom of the tin.

1. Put the tin onto baking parchment. Draw around it and cut out the shape. Grease the tin and put the paper in the bottom.

2. Sift the flour, mixed spice and salt through a sieve into a large bowl. Cut the butter into cubes and add it to the bowl.

3. Using your fingertips, rub in the butter until the mixture looks like breadcrumbs. Stir in the caster sugar and yeast.

Pour the beaten egg
mixture into the bowl.
everything with a
wooden spoon until you
make a dough.

5. Sprinkle some flour onto
a clean, dry work surface.
Then, knead the dough
by pushing it away from
you with both hands.

Carry on until the
dough is smooth
and springy.

6. Fold the dough in half
and turn it around.
Knead it again. Do this
for five minutes, then put
it into a greased bowl.

Cover the bowl with
plastic foodwrap. Leave
in a warm place for an
hour, until the dough has
risen to twice its size.

Knead in the
fruit for a
couple of
minutes.

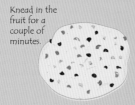

8. Turn the dough out of
the bowl and sprinkle the
dried fruit over it. Knead
the fruit into the dough
until it is mixed in.

9. Put the dough in the tin
and cover the tin with
plastic foodwrap. Put it in
a warm place for about 45
minutes to rise some more.

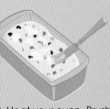

Heat your oven. Brush
the top of the dough with
milk, then put the tin in
the oven and bake the
bread for 30-35 minutes.

Remove the baking
parchment.

11. Push a skewer into the
loaf. If it comes out clean,
the loaf is cooked. Take
the loaf out of the tin. Put
it on a wire rack to cool.

Use a teaspoon to
drizzle the icing
onto the loaf.

12. Sift the icing sugar into
a bowl and mix in the
lemon juice. Drizzle the
icing over the loaf, then
scatter the cherries on top.

Spiced Easter biscuits

To make about 25 biscuits, you will need:

1 medium egg
100g (4oz) butter, softened
75g (3oz) caster sugar
200g (7oz) plain flour
½ teaspoon of ground cinnamon
½ teaspoon of ground ginger
50g (2oz) currants
5 teaspoons milk
about 2 tablespoons
  caster sugar to sprinkle

a 6cm (2½in) fluted cookie
  cutter
two greased baking sheets

Heat your oven to 200°C,
400°F, gas mark 6.

The biscuits need to be stored
in an airtight container and eaten
within five days.

1. Carefully break the egg
on the edge of a small
bowl, and pour it slowly
onto a saucer. Then, put
an egg cup over the yolk.

You will use
the egg white
later.

2. Hold the egg cup over
the yolk and tip the
saucer over the small
bowl, so that the egg
white dribbles into it.

Use a wooden
spoon.

Find out
how to make
cellophane
bags for your
biscuits on
page 63.

3. Put the butter and sugar
into a large bowl and
beat them until they are
creamy. Then, add the
egg yolk and beat it in.

Using a sieve, sift the [flo]ur, cinnamon and [gi]nger into the bowl. [Th]en, add the currants [an]d the milk too.

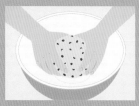

5. Mix everything together with a spoon, then squeeze the mixture with your hands until you have made a dough.

6. Wrap the dough in plastic foodwrap. Put it in the fridge for 20 minutes. Then, sprinkle a clean work surface with flour.

[Sp]rinkle flour [on] a rolling pin.

Heat your oven. Then, [p]ut the dough onto the [w]ork surface and roll it [o]ut until it is about 5mm [(¼]in) thick.

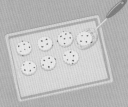

8. Use the cutter to cut out lots of biscuits. Then, carefully lift the biscuits onto the baking sheets, using a fish slice.

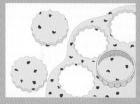

9. Squeeze the scraps of dough together to make a ball. Then, roll the dough out as you did before and cut out more biscuits.

[U]se a pastry brush.

[10]. Using a fork, beat the [e]gg white for a few [se]conds until it is frothy. [Br]ush a little egg white on [th]e top of each biscuit.

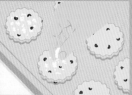

11. Sprinkle a little caster sugar over each biscuit. Bake them in the oven for 12-15 minutes. They will turn golden brown.

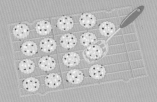

12. Leave the biscuits on the baking sheets for about five minutes. Then, lift them onto a wire rack and leave them to cool.

Easter daisy biscuits

To make about 50 biscuits, you will need:

75g (3oz) icing sugar
150g (5oz) butter, softened
a lemon
225g (8oz) plain flour
writing icing
small sweets and silver cake-decorating balls
a flower-shaped cookie cutter
two greased baking sheets

Heat your oven to 180°C, 350°F, gas mark 4.

The biscuits need to be stored in an airtight container and eaten within three days.

Use a sieve.

1. Sift the icing sugar into a large bowl. Add the butter and mix everything together with a spoon until the mixture is creamy.

2. Grate the rind from the lemon using the medium holes on a grater. Then, add the rind to the bowl and mix everything again.

Use a lemon squeezer.

Sprinkle some flour on a rolling pin too.

3. Cut the lemon in half and squeeze the juice from it. Then, stir a tablespoon of lemon juice into the creamy mixture.

4. Sift the flour through a sieve into the bowl. Mix it in until you make a smooth dough. Then, wrap the dough in plastic foodwrap.

5. Put the dough in a fridge for 30 minutes, to become firmer. Then, sprinkle some flour onto a clean work surface.

6. Heat your oven. Then, roll out the dough until it is about 5mm (¼in) thick. Cut out lots of flower shapes, using the cutter.

This recipe makes 50 biscuits this size. The number of biscuits depends on the size of your cutter.

7. Put the flower shapes onto the baking sheets. Squeeze the scraps into a ball, then roll it out again and cut out more shapes.

The biscuits should be lightly browned.

8. Bake the biscuits for 15 minutes. Leave them on the baking sheets for two minutes, then put them on a wire rack to cool.

9. When the biscuits are cool, decorate them with icing. Draw lines, swirls and dots. Press sweets into the middle of the icing.

Cheesy chicks

To make about 15 chicks, you will need:

75g (3oz) mature Cheddar cheese
100g (4oz) plain flour
50g (2oz) butter, refrigerated
the yolk from a medium egg
5 teaspoons cold water
a chick-shaped or other cookie cutter
two greased baking sheets

Heat your oven to 190°C, 375°F,
gas mark 5.

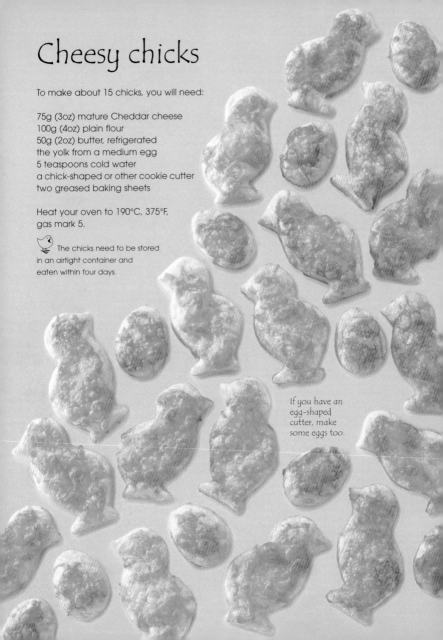 The chicks need to be stored
in an airtight container and
eaten within four days.

If you have an
egg-shaped
cutter, make
some eggs too.

Use the
the holes
a grater.

1. Grate the cheese. Sift the flour through a sieve into a large bowl. Then, cut the butter into chunks and add it to the bowl.

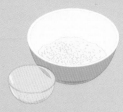

2. Mix in the butter until it is coated in flour. Rub it in with your fingers, until it looks like breadcrumbs. Add half of the cheese.

3. Mix the egg yolk and water in a small bowl. Put 2 teaspoonfuls in a cup, then pour the rest over the flour mixture.

4. Stir everything together, then squeeze the mixture until you make a smooth dough. Make it a slightly flattened round shape.

5. Wrap the dough in plastic foodwrap and put it in a fridge to chill for 30 minutes. While it is in the fridge, heat your oven.

6. Sprinkle flour onto a clean work surface and a rolling pin. Roll out the dough until it is about 5mm (¹⁄₄in) thick.

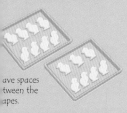

Leave spaces between the shapes.

7. Use the cutter to cut out thick shapes. Put them onto the baking sheets. Squeeze the scraps into a ball, then roll them out.

8. Cut out more shapes. Brush the tops of the shapes with the egg mixture, then sprinkle them with grated cheese.

Use a fish slice.

9. Bake the chicks for 12 minutes. Leave them on the baking sheets for five minutes, then put them on a wire rack to cool.

Boxes and bags

Bunny boxes

This side of the head needs to be on the fold.

1. Carefully cut the top off a tissue box and paint the box. Find a piece of thick paper the same colour. Fold the paper in half.

2. Draw half of a bunny's head, like this. Keeping the paper folded, cut out the shape. Open out the paper and flatten it.

3. Draw a face. Then, glu̇ the head onto one end o̓ the box. Glue a piece of cotton wool onto the opposite end, for a tail.

Pretty sweets

Pile sweets or biscuits into a bunny box as an Easter gift.

1. Cut a square of thin cellophane that is bigger than the sweet, like this. Then, put the sweet in the middle of the square.

2. Wrap the cellophane around the sweet and tape it. Tie a piece of parcel ribbon around each end of the sweet.

Sweetie bags

Leave long ends on the ribbon.

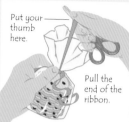

Put your thumb here.

Pull the end of the ribbon.

1. Carefully cut a square of thin cellophane. Then, place some biscuits or sweets onto the middle of the square.

2. Gather up the edges of the square and tie a piece of parcel ribbon around the cellophane, above the biscuits.

3. To make the ribbon curl, hold it between your thumb and the blade of some closed scissors, and pull it firmly.

Add a paper handle to a box to make a basket.

Save food boxes and wrap ribbons around them.

Easter tags

1. Draw a rectangle on a piece of white card with a wax crayon. Then, draw the body of a chick with a yellow crayon.

Draw an egg shape and fill it with lines and patterns.

2. Add a beak, a leg and an eye. Paint over the picture with runny paint. The crayon lines will show through the paint.

You can fill different areas with different colours of paint, like this flower.

3. When the paint is dry, cut around the rectangle, leaving a painted edge. Tape a piece of ribbon to the back of the tag.